EYES ON THE STARS

WRITER CHAPS – SEASON ONE

SHORT BOOKS FULL OF OUTSTANDING ADVICE FROM AUSTRALIA'S TOP SPECULATIVE FICTION WRITERS

You Are Not Your Writing and Other Sage Advice, Angela Slatter

From Baby Brain To Writer Brain: Writing Through A World of Parenting Distractions, Tansy Rayner Roberts

Eyes on the Stars: Writing Science Fiction & Fantasy, Sean Williams

The Martial Art of Writing and Other Essays, Alan Baxter

Trapping Ghosts on the Page, Kaaron Warren

EYES ON THE STARS

Writing Science Fiction and Fantasy

SEAN WILLIAMS

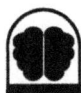

Brain Jar Press
PO Box 6687
Upper Mt Gravatt, QLD, 4122
Australia
www.BrainJarPress.com

Cover design by Peter Ball
Cover Image: Astronaut in Fantasy World, Sergey Nivens/Shutterstock

ISBN: 978-1-922479-02-0

A Day in the Life of...

WITH THANKS TO KATE ELTHAM & KIM WILKINS

This is the story of a very odd couple. Like all relationships between identical siblings, theirs is an uneasy one. The Pro is slim, well dressed, and immaculately groomed — or likes to think he is, anyway — with a penchant for black. His older brother, the Geek, tends to shab about in tracksuit pants and t-shirts, and is somehow never quite the right weight. That they coexist at all is quite remarkable, given their disparate tendencies. It doesn't take more than a casual glance to reveal that they are complete opposites in almost every respect.

The Pro thinks of himself as a Writer, with a capital W. He has a set routine he follows every day, and is proud of his output not just in terms of quantity but quality as well. He takes great care to be both reliable and personable, believing those two traits to be the cornerstones of professionalism. He strives to marry the fickle art of his muse with the demands of a steady career, knowing that the former is only fickle of you let it be, and that one sets one's *own* demands, no one else. A career is successful only on its own terms. No matter how many awards one might win or books one might sell, if writing doesn't allow one to lead an independent life, or doesn't satisfy the inner critic, then it's not successful at all.

The Geek, on the other hand, is a Scribbler, with a capital S. Ideas take him off on wild turns of speculation, derailing deadlines and upsetting schedules. While the Pro works his way through a carefully plotted synopsis, chapter by chapter, counting his 1500 words a day with all the miserliness of a tax collector, the Geek is a puppy snapping at butterflies, scampering after the ideas that will not go into the present book, or even the next book, but the book after that. They might not be suitable for a book at all, but something completely inappropriate like a feature script, a graphic novel, a computer game. When inspiration strikes him, he is off, grinning with delight at the wonder-laden fields of his own internal landscape.

The Pro disapproves of such behaviour. He knows the value of ideas — indeed, his career rests on them — but he also knows that going at them in such a fashion gets one nowhere. Back in the early days, when they first shared an office, the Pro would sometimes let the Geek follow his nose, trusting in his scruffier sibling's instinct for a Good Idea to lead them somewhere fruitful. Numerous disappointments, however, taught him the error of relying too much on that particular approach. The Geek had the joy of a puppy — and the attention span, too. No sooner would he find something genuinely interesting than he would be off in a completely different direction, barking like a loon. Putting the Geek in front of a word processor in that state resulted only in brilliant opening paragraphs that dwindled into disconnected phrases, and ultimately nothing.

The Pro cannot afford false starts. If his career is to remain afloat, he must maintain a steady output, never pursuing too many ideas or too few. While he sneers at the thought of a job in the field he studied at university — Economics — he can see the sense in a carefully managed strategy for success. He has a ten-year plan.

The Geek sometimes despairs for his older brother. He lives for the Flow, the Rush, and the Fire. He remembers the good old days when, seized suddenly by a Great Idea, he would drop whatever he was doing and write for hours on end until a short story was finished, consuming nothing but coffee and cigarettes, sustained only by the sheer joy of Story. These days, the Flow is doled out in neat rations: never so much as to leave him utterly exhausted, as in those wild, heady days, but never so little that he loses interest. He feels like a junkie, or a donkey eternally lunging for the carrot. His hunger is never quite satiated.

THERE IS a peculiar method to their madness. Keith Tyson, winner of the 2002 Turner Prize, said in *New Scientist*:

'As an artist, you turn yourself into a 24-hour art developer, so you cannot pinpoint the precise moment [when an idea arises, when you are creating]. It is like asking when the Second World War started. The creative process is just an attitude...

"[It's] very hard to describe the creative process because often you are just messing around, thinking, doodling.'

The Geek is the doodler, the time-waster. He'll spend all day reading magazines or surfing the web, justifying it as passive research, while the Pro nags and scolds him from the sidelines, where he is slowly and steadily winning the race. Nevertheless, the Geek is also capable of blinding feats of inspiration. When an idea strikes him, he is off his mark like an Olympic sprinter, leaving the Pro lagging behind.

Tyson went on to say: 'The artist is portrayed as a half-mad, half-creative person, and the scientist in a similar vein. One thing that drives the whole process in the studio — and in the lab — is the effort to remain curious, to remain a 14-year-old. Everything is interesting if you look hard enough.'

The Geek, reading this, feels that he has found a kindred spirit. While his stuffy younger brother agonises about finding public acceptance, he just gets on with doing what he loves, in a world that he finds absolutely, endlessly fascinating.

The Pro is sympathetic. In fact, he agrees with Tyson on every point. Being a writer is indeed a 24-hour effort. It is hard work and not something one does when the mood takes hold. The Geek is a frequent victim of writers' block; this is the flipside of his intuitive, haphazard approach. What will they do if the block sticks longer than a day or two? How will they eat if they don't meet their many deadlines?

As their profile has increased, demands on their time have increased too. Being a full-time writer isn't just about writing. It's a job like any other, with its demands and opportunities. Between the two of them, the Geek and the Pro have to juggle the books and the phone, alternating roles of secretary, accountant, manager, webmaster, researcher, housekeeper, and chef. The shopping won't be done on its own. The garden will die while they're on tour if no one looks after it. They've learned the hard way that one can't survive on junk food alone. Sleep isn't just dead time: it has a powerful recuperative value without which everything falters. (And it brings the occasional flashes of inspiration, too.)

Far from their study confining them, the last two years has been a veritable whirlwind of travel. The Geek and the

Pro have been invited to every state writers' festival in the country at least once and have attended all the major genre conferences, where possible. They have travelled to Los Angeles — where the Pro got to look especially stylish in a brand-new tuxedo — and will shortly be going around the world on a non-stop schmooze-fest. They have averaged one flight a week and have totalled up more nights away from home than in it. Yet the Pro still strives to maintain his output. He has finished two novels already this year — one of which went on to be a NY Times bestseller — and is already halfway through another. He whips out his laptop at the slightest opportunity: in planes, airport lounges, hotel rooms, cafes. He is a quick-draw scribe egging his brother on, whenever a creative noon might fall.

His brother is no slouch either. The Geek may look like he's sightseeing, but he's actually soaking up the environment around him, absorbing ideas. He doesn't know what he'll need or how he'll use it, but he does know that keeping one's eyes and mind open is a sure-fire way to happen upon inspiration. If you could take his method out of his head and give it flesh, it would be a fly-fisher casting over and over into the mighty world-river. If you ever notice the Geek staring blankly into the middle distance, chances are the fly-fisher in his head has caught something.

THE PRO IS A WORRIER, but he gets things done. The Geek knows he doesn't worry enough, but he gets by in the end. Between the two of them, they strike a kind of balance. Both have strengths and weaknesses; together they can take advantage of the former and make up for the latter.

The Geek loves hearing from fans, but he feels uncomfortable seeking praise when it hasn't been offered.

The Pro is the one who actually answers fan mail, because the Geek is not a good letter writer. The Pro is the one who deals with editors and agents, but in the end it's usually the Geek who does the work of fixing the problems. While the Pro is off setting up deals and scheduling the next project, the Geek is slaving away at the keyboard, adding one final layer of pizzazz to the story he started months ago. They both have mixed feelings towards their brag shelf, the place in which they display every book and magazine in which they have appeared. The Geek sometimes stares at it in awe, wondering how on Earth he managed to get *here* — where he dreamed of being all his life. Surely it couldn't have happened to little old him! The Pro is intensely proud of their achievements, aware of the hard work and determination it took to get here, but knows he can't afford to rest on his laurels. The moment they start to take anything for granted, to get too comfortable, that's the moment it'll all be pulled out from under them.

There is one area on which they totally agree, and that concerns community. This may surprise those who know the Geek best, for he is not a natural party person. He's the one standing in a corner by a pot plant, crinkling a plastic cup in one sweaty hand, afraid of being set adrift, of sinking. The Pro, on the other hand, is gregarious and charming. He loves a good party, and he loves to gossip. He is found flitting from conversation to conversation, smiling and cracking jokes, downing numerous glasses of champagne and accepting compliments with cool self-deprecation, while the Geek scans the party for people he knows and likes, and sticks to the first one he finds.

Both the Pro and the Geek genuinely love people, although they go about expressing that affection in very different ways. They both depend on the community around them for support and friendship. Without their friends in the business, they would never have come this far. The Geek may get a little too excited about Dr Who and Star Wars sometimes, but he is pleased to learn that many of his colleagues display exactly the same social faux pas, when egged on a little. The Pro learns from his friends that they often share the same concerns as he for their careers, their industries, their futures. The existence of the community and their participation in it ensures that they never feel alone, as they did in the early days. Writing *is* a solitary pursuit, but it doesn't have to be a lonely one.

Friends in the business are only half the story. The Geek and the Pro have learned the hard way that, although writing is their vocation and arguably the most important thing in their lives, it shouldn't dominate their lives completely. A balance is important. Maintaining a social life was extremely difficult in the early days — when writing wasn't earning much money and they had to work numerous part-time jobs to pay the rent — but with no one else to talk to but each other, they quickly go stir-crazy. Crazy doesn't always mean brilliant, or even saleable, so it's no way to plan for a career, let alone to be terribly happy. The Geek and the Pro are careful now to make time to maintain a social life in order to stay at least nominally sane. This is another reason why the Pro likes his daily word-count target: not only does meeting it ensure that he maintains a steady output of workable prose, but it tells him when he can let himself *stop*. Without that benchmark, he might diligently work on into the wee hours without pause, or feel constantly guilty that he wasn't doing enough. Neither is good for his stress levels.

Together, despite the odds, the Geek and the Pro weather bad reviews and unexpected setbacks unflustered. Deep down they know that, despite their differences, they are stronger for their collaboration. Without the Pro's determined professionalism, they would never have finished their first novel; without the Geek's wide-eyed optimism, the mountain of rejections would soon have overwhelmed them both. When the parties stop and it's time to go back into the study, the Geek and the Pro settle back into their familiar routine and get on with what they do best.

The Writer's Career Path

WITH THANKS TO KIRSTY BROOKS AND TIM POWERS

There are lots of different possible career paths for writers. None of them are 100% right or 100% wrong; there is no correct way to be successful. What *is* success, anyway? Is it having a short story published, or a novel? Is it getting a grant or appearing on a bestseller list? Is it being able to support yourself by writing alone or seeing someone read one of your books on a plane?

Decide what sort of writer you want to be. Maybe you already know; maybe you're still working it out. It may take a while for you to hit on the thing that particularly appeals to you, or matches your skills. There's no shame in not knowing yet.

People who write books don't only write novels. They also write short story collections, anthologies of poems, biographies, autobiographies (although this assumes you're famous already), textbooks, literary non-fiction, and so on.

Writers also write government reports, advertising and copywriting, newsletters, journalism (TV, radio, internet/reporting news, articles, etc), reviewing, board games, computer game manuals, scripts for TV and movies, and more.

Writers work in such fields as manuscript assessment, CV writing, grant application services, editing, publishing, teaching, tutoring, mentoring, etc.

There are many opportunities to earn money using your writing skills and see your words in print. You can be all of these things, or just one of them. You're most likely to be many of them in the course of your career, but you might have just one you particularly aspire to.

Me, it's writing novels. That's what I want to do, so everything I do is geared towards that end. If I can't make a living from writing novels, or if I stop enjoying writing them, then I have failed. Those are the terms on which I measure my personal success — not anyone else's. My talk today will be biased towards that kind of thinking, but the principles can be extended across all areas of writing.

I divide the process of getting published into three phases. The first addresses issues someone at the beginning of their career should consider. The second is aimed at the author of one or more unsold mss. The third focuses on what happens after a book is published. There are, most likely, many other things an author should consider at these and other stages of their career. Knowledge in all these areas does not necessarily guarantee success.

I'm not going to lie to you. There are no secret handshakes or rules that will get you on your particular dream-path. If there was, we'd all be on our own already. If you want to be a successful writer, be prepared to have to make up most of it as you go along.

You also have to be prepared to work as hard, and as long, as if you wanted to be a violinist in an orchestra, a professional cricketer or a doctor. Occasionally, someone will write a book and get it published straight away, but that's pretty unusual.

I believe that there's always hope, but that there are no guarantees. Don't EXPECT success or you're bound to be disappointed.

This doesn't have to be depressing. It can be empowering too — I certainly found it so. If hard work is all that separates the wannabes from the pros, then that's cool. I can work hard! I love writing, after all; and if I don't give this, my dream, everything I've got, then I'll feel like I'm letting myself down.

———

OKAY. Here goes. It may seem that I've gone right back to basics, and in a way I have. But remember that there is no well-defined path for each novel, or even for each writer. Phases One to Three overlap constantly. At any given time, I'm doing all three, so I need to keep the basic principles in mind, and so do you.

PHASE ONE: PRODUCING SOMETHING THAT HAS A HOPE OF SELLING

To have a successful career as a writer, you have to write the best story you possibly can, for the genre you're writing in.

Does this sound mercenary? I don't think so. If you want to be a *professional* writer, you have to sell your work. There's simply no way around that, which means you have to take into account the needs of the people who are buying (editors and/or the readers).

That doesn't mean that you can't write what you love — far from it. That's the *most* important thing! But there might be many different things you love to write, or at least several.

If you are determined only to write ghost stories set on the South Australian coast during the years 1800 – 1810, be aware that you are making it harder for yourself. Not impossible. Just harder. Do it anyway, if you must.

Here are some things you can do to help you along the way. Some of them should be self-explanatory; I mention them now to highlight how important they are. If you're not doing them already, you should be.

- **Read** - A writer reads, the more the better. If you're not interested in storytelling, what makes you think you can tell a story? Read widely and learn the craft as you go (like one of those subliminal tapes people used to play under their pillows to help them give up smoking).
- **Write** - A writer writes. Most of the writers I know were writing as children, teenager, adults. They would do it even if they had another job (and many of them *do* have other jobs). If you want to be a writer, just do it. No excuses. You don't find time to write: you *make* it.
- **Research** - Just about anything counts as research. Flicking through magazines at your doctor's surgery; talking to people on the street; keeping your eyes open as you walk around. Take something you can write on with you everywhere and write down everything that sparks your imagination.
- **Efficiency** - Ideas come at weird times and can be easily forgotten (hence the importance of taking notes). Research maximizes your chances of having ideas; reading will show you how other writers have dealt with their ideas; writing — lots of it — will help you work out, slowly but surely, what

ideas are ready to go into a story. You can't use everything. Not everything you start will finish well. Polish your instincts in order to tell when your sticking with something that will get somewhere as opposed to doodling around the edges of your career.

- **Revise** - don't just send out your first draft. Get perspective on it any way you can — put it in a drawer for a month; read it aloud; change the fonts and lay-out; send it out to beta readers — then do everything you must to make it the best piece of prose you've ever produced. Because that's what you want to end up on your future editor's desk, not something you knocked off at the bus stop while waiting to go to uni. Bear in mind that good enough is not good at all. Good enough is *bad*.

These are the first steps on your career path — steps you will keep taking over and over as you progress. Like a child learning to walk, practice makes perfect. Skipping one of these steps is risking disaster, or at least wasting your time.

There are other, specific exercises you can set yourself. It's not necessary to do all of these things, but they will help you step out of your "writer-as-writer" shoes and address the business side of your potential career.

- Name your genre or target audience. If you imagine your work published, how does it look in your mind? Where does it sit on the shelves? What sort of covers do they have? (Don't be afraid of terms like "sci-fi" or "romance." If the cap fits, wear it with pride.)
- Name three authors who publish in your genre.

(You should know without having to look them up.
You should be reading widely in the field.)

- Has anyone else attempted to cover this particular
corner of your genre before? Are you sufficiently
aware of their work to explain why yours is
different?
- Name two outstanding examples of work in your
field and explain what makes them good.
- Name two poor examples of work in your field
and explain what makes them bad.
- Name three organisations that offer writing-
related courses that might improve your skills (and
will look good on your CV).
- Describe in one concise and interesting sentence
what your work is about. (This will come in handy
at parties or family gatherings, if nowhere else.)
- How many projects do you have in the pipeline,
and what are they?

The next two points require absolute honesty:

- Can you describe, briefly, why you want to write,
and what you feel you have to offer?
- Where do you see yourself in ten years?

The answers to any of these questions will shape the path
before you, and the ways you go about finding it through the
undergrowth.

PHASE TWO: POSITIONING YOUR WORK SO IT INCREASES ITS CHANCES OF SELLING

Here I have to reiterate that there are no right answers, just
lots of opinions.

Some specific exercises, to start with.

- Earlier, you named your genre. Now name three publishing houses/imprints/magazines that publish in your genre.
- Name three agents who represent authors in your field. What are their reputations like? (There are agents who genuinely want to help writers, and then there are sharks circling, homing in on the slightest scent of neediness. You know who you want to be with.)
- What are the submission guidelines for the above places? Do you know how they prefer to see the manuscript (ms) on the page? Do you know what information they like to see accompanying an ms?
- Name the person to whom you will address your submission in order that it will be read promptly (ie. commissioning editor, reader, etc). If you don't know their name, find out. (Cold-calling is fine. Just keep it businesslike.)
- Write a *brief* covering letter to accompany your submission.
- Write a one-page synopsis of your novel. Include the end.
- Write a 100-word bio.
- Write a short (writing-related) CV. (Only give the people you're submitting to what they ask for. Don't burden them with stuff they neither want nor need.)
- Write an application to your local funding body for assistance with your next project.
- Where is your nearest Writers' Centre? Can they help you with any of the above?

- Have you considered ms assessment? If so, name two reputable ones.
- Join the ASA, SFWA, whatever organisation is relevant. Don't be afraid to ask for advice.

Some of the answers to these questions can be found on the web. Some of them can't. The ones that can't depend on your integration within the industry. Remember: you don't have to have a book in print to talk to people. You can go to workshops, to writers' festivals, to signings. You can buy books on writing. You can join writers' groups. The important thing is that you're *talking* to the people who are, or might one day, be your peers, and *listening* to what they tell you. At least half of everything I know about writing — which isn't even close to being exhaustive — came from listening to writers, editors, publishers, agents, sales reps, and so on. (The rest, as an aside, I learned by making mistakes.)

For example: agents. Kim Stanley Robinson told me in Hobart, 1995: 'Ask five writers their opinion on agents and you'll get five different answers.' It's true. My opinion, for the record, is that you don't necessarily need one here in Australia, but you definitely need one for the US and the rest of the world. You need one in New York, and you need one who won't charge you to read your ms. (This is important: in traditional publishing, money should always flow to the author, not the other way around.)

But if you ask other authors, they might tell you different things. It's up to you to sort through the information you receive and come up with an answer that makes sense to you. Coming to an informed decision — which is what you want, not one plucked out of the ether or at random — requires getting that information. The best way to get it — on agents, publishers, editors, and others of that ilk — is where it's not in print and therefore not possibly libellous.

Regarding agents again, the only thing I can say with any degree of certainty is that if you offer an agent money, you stand a good chance of becoming a client. But choose wisely. As Tim Powers says: 'Picking an agent is like picking a spouse — better to have none than to have one that's not perfect.'

Another important thing to realise is that, as soon as you send your work out in the mail, you're becoming a career writer. You're on the path. If you never send it out, you are not a professional. You're just filling empty time. The same applies to self-publishing: if you never actually *publish* anything, what is it you're doing, exactly?

Even if you don't *feel* like you're a professional writer, you still have to act like one. Here are some things you can do to make it easier. They're like the kit you'll carry on your path, if you like — although that might be stretching the metaphor too far.

- Format your ms correctly. Counter-intuitively, it's not supposed to look like it would in print. It's supposed to look like it was typed on a 1950s manual typewriter. I know it doesn't make any sense; do it anyway. (Once you have a relationship with an editor, maybe then you can send in your mss printed on both sides of pink paper in single font 8-point Matisse, but never without asking first.)[1]
- Most publishers and agents prefer sample chapters and outline. They won't *buy* from an unknown on that basis—they'll ask for the full ms first—but they are more likely to glance at several small

submissions in their spare time than take on a single giant file.

- The outline you send with your ms isn't the outline you work from. This one is all in present tense, has no "style," and shouldn't be more than five pages — ten at the most.
- Always spell-and grammar-check before it goes in the mail. *Always.*
- Be prepared to wait six months or more for a reply. Unsolicited mss may languish even longer. Delays are industry standard; get used to them if you can (I'm still trying). Don't nag.
- Attend conventions if you can afford them and enjoy meeting people; don't *expect* that they will help your career, and don't act too needy. Don't stand copies of your book in front of you in panels. Don't force yourself onto editors. Don't start up or prolong a conversation about your own work. Don't laugh too loudly at an editor's jokes. Whatever you do, don't' tell an editor that you think you can be a writer because of all the trash that gets published. (They may be responsible for some of the trash.)
- Become part of the community. And there *is* a community. Everybody knows and talks to everybody; that's how we survive, through a constant recycling of support and advice. From the outside in, it might look like it's an elite club or a conspiracy. The truth is, there's no "out" or "in" at all. There are just people who have similar interests and want similar things. There's room for all of us.
- Lastly, invest in an office — desk, good comfortable chair, photocopier, fax machine,

laptop etc. Don't worry about feeling like a fake/
You've got to do it at some point, so, like a lot of
this stuff, it's best to pick up the skills early.

PHASE THREE: POSITIONING *YOU* SO YOU HAVE A CHANCE OF SELLING

Before you're published, getting published is the big hurdle.
Then suddenly you're over that hurdle and tripping over new
ones you didn't even suspect were there.

We are in even more nebulous territory here. You can get
advice on deals and contracts from your agent or from the
ASA, so I won't dwell too much on that side of things.
Basically, you should be aware of the rights you're selling,
and you shouldn't be too pushy about money. We're usually
not talking squillions for a first — or sometimes tenth —
novel. Be realistic. Your talks with other writers should fill
you in on this.

As soon as your book is sold, there are a series of things
you have to consider. You should, in fact, have been thinking
about them long before now. They won't necessarily make
your writing any better, but they will make you a better
writer. Because that's what you are, once you've made a sale.
You can legitimately say that you are *a writer*, not writing.

Exercises:

- Write a 100-word cover copy for your novel.
- Name three bookshops that carry books in your genre, and name the managers or buyers of those stores. (The chances are, if you're a good reader, you'll know them already.)
- Are you aware of any professional organisations related to or representing your field? What benefits do they offer you?

- Name three radio programs that might be interested in your work, for review or promotion. What about television, magazines, newspapers, bloggers?
- Name two journalists who review your genre.
- Name three venues or organisations that conduct or promote public readings.
- Investigate other authors' websites. What features do they possess that appeal to you?
- Design your own website or pay someone to do it for you.
- Name three organisations that regularly require writers of any kind — ie. advertisers, web-site designers, magazine publishers, etc. (I put this in as a nod to those sensible people who are prepared to do more than just write novels for a living.)

There are certain things that writers are expected to do. They are expected to help the publisher promote their book. They are expected to work productively and politely with an editor. They are expected to deliver on time. They are expected to write more than one book, in a timely fashion. (Publishers buy writers, not books. So the saying goes.) They are expected to keep their audience satisfied. They are expected to, well, write.

A publisher, in turn, will do its best to make your book look suitable for the market, promote your book, deliver your advances and royalties in a timely fashion. They will also try, within the limited scope of their powers, to nurture you as a writer. That really isn't their job, though. It's yours.

(While on the subject of editors, remember that they are uniformly overworked and underpaid. They also know a lot more about writing and the marketplace than you do, and they're usually right. Consider carefully every point your editor makes. Where you reject an editorial suggestion, make sure there's a good reason for it.)

In the perfect world, your book is published, its sales are good, and you sell your publishers another one just like it. And another one. And so on, into the sunset. Phases One to Three keep on cycling around and overlapping, and everyone's happy.

It often doesn't work out that way, though. When things go wrong, the Writer's Career Path can take on some decidedly convoluted shapes. Like any well-oiled machines, things only get more interesting — and irritating — when they break down.

DAMAGE CONTROL

Things always go wrong. Expect it, and try to get used to it. Some disasters will be completely outside your control; some will happen because you were *in* control and either you made a mistake or were just plain ornery.

For starters, you are going to get bad reviews and rejections. Assume it; everyone gets them. *Never* respond; not when reviewers get basic details wrong or correct you on points where you were accurate, or when they seem to be talking about a whole different book or insulting your boyfriend. Don't take them to heart.

As Neil Gaiman once said: 'The best reaction to a rejection slip is a sort of wild-eyed madness, an evil grin, and sitting yourself in front of the keyboard muttering "Okay, you bastards. Try rejecting this!" and then writing something so unbelievably brilliant that all other writers will disembowel themselves with their pens upon reading it, because there's nothing left to write.'

Do that.

Here are some things you might have to deal with and

some ways to deal with them. Every situation should be decided on its merit, after consultation with your agent, your peers, your loved-ones, your lawyer. If you've considered the very basic issues of what sort of writer you want to be and how you intend to go about it, you should be able to adapt to all sorts of situations. (You are, of course, entitled to change your mind at any time.) I don't have all the answers. No one does.

- **Changing genres:** As someone who likes jumping around, I say go for it. *Provided* you keep your original audience satisfied, you can do what you want. Look at Iain (M) Banks: he did both, but only because he wasn't skimping in either genre. I have to write twice as much because I want to write fantasy as well as science fiction. Quality or quantity, if you've got either you might be able to get away with it.
- **Applying for grants:** Someone asked me recently if a science fiction application stood less of a chance with the Literature Board of the Australia Council *just because* it's science fiction. The answer is 'no' (and I speak from an informed position, having been a peer assessor for the Board *and* received two grants from them). All you have to do is meet their guidelines and be ahead of the rest of the pack, which is as hard for speculative fiction as it is for any other genre. Apply every year, no matter how many times they knock you back, because just one successful application can make a big difference to your career.
- **Writing YA/adult/middle-grade fiction at the same time:** The same with writing for other

genres. Follow your heart — and your head. Be aware that there's a certain risk in bouncing between audiences but there are ways to minimise that risk. Seek advice from those that do it well.

- **Creating pseudonyms:** If your career goes down the toilet, or just stalls, or if you want to write splatterpunk novels as well as Victorian romances, then using a pseudonym is an option. It's not necessarily a bad thing. Some writers believe that using a pseudonym frees them up, psychologically, to do things they wouldn't normally do under their own name.
- **Being orphaned:** When your editor leaves your publisher and you're left with someone who doesn't like your work — or, perhaps worse, is completely indifferent to it and your fate — then you have been orphaned. This can be problematic and must be handled delicately. There are ways of doing it without getting everyone offside, and your agent can help you with that. Again, seek advice relevant to your specific situation.
- **Writing for more than one publisher:** Can be a conflict of interest, but isn't always. I've had four publishers here in Australia and as many in the States, and it's never caused a problem. Not one that couldn't be sorted out, anyway, by keeping everyone informed at all times. As long as you deliver what you've said you will, no one has any right to be offended.
- **Public appearances:** Are a good idea, but how much of them you do, and of what type, that's up to you. Self-promotion takes time; if you'd rather be writing than caravanning around country Australia, speaking at every public library and

every school, then I don't blame you — but I know a number of authors whose careers have been helped by such activities. I feel guilty, sometimes, for not doing more of it. Find your own balance. Don't do anything you aren't good at, and do be open to occasionally trying new things.

- **Saying 'no'**: The hardest lesson I've had to learn is to say 'no' to stuff. Obviously there are things you just *have* to say 'yes' to—if they match your desired career choices—but there are times when you really shouldn't let yourself be distracted from what you signed on for.

A writer's career will necessarily have some ups and down, even if we might hate it to be so. For every possible situation, there are a number of possible responses. I dream sometimes of a smooth and simple ride to fame and riches, but I know that's unrealistic. I expect it to go awry every now and again, so I'm not going to get disappointed. At the very least, I'll be emotionally ready for whatever comes, and at best I'll be pleasantly surprised.

Make your own path (which is a very Zen thing to say) and don't forget to report in every now and again, so we know where it's taking you.

Lastly, don't be afraid to dream big. Dream small and, well, what do you expect will happen? You might succeed by accident, but you won't be prepared for success. Dreams (and imagination) are the primate's way of preparing for things that haven't happened yet. Be prepared. Be bold. Be brave.

---

1. Ooooh Ouch! Not unless you want to buy me new Xtra magnifying glasses... LOL...

The Delicate* Art of Media Tie-Ins

WITH THANKS TO KEVIN J. ANDERSON

(* SOME MIGHT SAY DUBIOUS.)

The novelisation or media tie-in novel is a much benighted phenomenon. I find this quite strange, and not just because I once devoured them by the handful. They account for a large proportion of speculative book sales (walk into any book shop, stand before the metres of rack space devoted to Star Wars novels, and feel yourself turn as green as Greebo with envy) yet they are not reviewed, they are ignored by academia, and their very existence is regarded as anathema by many people in the industry. The complaint that tie-in novels "steal" readers from more "serious" works is a common and, I think, fallacious one. How many young people reading tie-ins would read at all if books related to their favourite media properties weren't available? How many of them go on to read other books after growing out of the tie-ins? Even if the answer to the first question is "none" and to the second, only "some", then the net return from tie-ins is still positive. They bring new readers to the field — and that's always a good thing.

Let's take a step back. What is a media tie-in novel? Where do they come from? The "media" part of the term refers to the source material on which the novel is based. This could be a movie (*Star Wars, Battlestar Galactica*), a TV show (*Star Trek, Doctor Who, Buffy*), a graphic novel or comic (*Batman, Superman*), or increasingly these days a computer game (*Halo, The Legend of Zelda*). Novels, too, spin-off tie-ins of their own: just look at all the publications surrounding the Harry Potter series and The Lord of the Rings. Anything that generates a demand for product above and beyond the existing work has the potential to generate tie-ins. We see it happen every day when novels become movies, movies become TV series, TV series become comics, comics become computer games, and so on. The permutations are endless.

When I was a wee lad, my franchise of choice was Doctor Who, and my appetite was insatiable. Video players were newfangled commodities in the 70s, so the only way I could revisit a favourite series was by reading the book based on it, literally taken word for word from the script with exposition added to turn it into a proper book. Such *novelisations* were, for me, a sort of playback system — one with full colour, perfect sound, and much better special effects.

These days, video players are commonplace, and we have DVD, Blu Ray, and cable TV as well. Who reads the book of the show when the show itself is right at your fingertips? Novelisations of scripts are still being written, but they tend to be of blockbuster movies and by blockbuster authors: *Star Wars Episode I: The Phantom Menace* by Terry Brooks is a perfect example. Or they are marketed as souvenirs, no different to t-shirts, soundtracks, action figures and the like.

That still leaves the tie-in novel, though, and sales of those are booming. A tie-in is a novel set in the universe of a popular franchise, usually featuring the same characters and situations. Want to know what happened to Han and Leia's romance after the credits rolled on *Return of the Jedi*? Read *The Courtship of Princess Leia* by Dave Wolverton. Want to know more about the history of Buffy's two favourite vampires? Read *Cursed* by Mel Odom. Want to know how Brian Kinney and Michael Novotney formed such a strong bond, then read *Every Nine Seconds: A Queer As Folk Novel* by Joseph Brockton.

I mention the latter to demonstrate that novelisations and tie-ins do not belong solely to the realm of science fiction and fantasy. While a lot of them certainly do, there are many exceptions, ranging from the Home Alone and Mary-Kate & Ashley franchises to the continuing adventures of Jackie Chan. Many of these are for young adult or child readers, but plenty of adults read them too.

There's obviously money in them thar hills. So how do you go about getting some? The first thing to know is that distance is not necessarily an obstacle. Shows may be made in Hollywood, but the books can be written anywhere. Several Australians have managed it in recent times: husband and wife team Jonathon Blum and Kate Orman have written several novels between them for the Doctor Who franchise (their co-written novel *Fallen Gods* was even nominated for an Aurealis and Ditmar Award); Russell Blackford is the author of *The New John Connor Chronicles* set in the Terminator universe; Garth Nix wrote a YA novelisation of the X-Files episode "The Calusari"; Shane Dix and I penned the Force Heretic Trilogy in The Star Wars: New Jedi Order series; I wrote the novelisation of *Star Wars: The Force Unleashed*; and more.

Some of these writers were already established novelists before writing for their respective franchises and secured their deals as a result of that work. For others, these books were their first published novels. If forced to generalize about their methods, I would have to say that the same principles apply to writing fiction for a franchise as apply to any other sort of fiction. Here are just some:

1) YOU'RE WRITING FOR A SPECIFIC MARKET

Knowing that market is crucial.

2) THERE ARE CERTAIN RULES OF GENRE YOU SIMPLY CAN'T BREAK

Every genre from romance to high lit has its established readership and its conventions. Not knowing either is courting disaster, or at least inviting disappointment home for dinner. The immediate advantage of writing for a franchise is that both are laid on the table right at the very start. You can't swear in Star Wars novels just as you can't have the Doctor murder their assistant. Trying will only end in tears.

3) YOU MUST BE PROFESSIONAL

By this I mean more than just coming across as an obsessed fan, although that too is important.

4) YOU NEED A GOOD AGENT

Franchise deals are very complicated, since they involve pre-existing properties, and their royalty rates (if any) vary. Best to have someone watching over your shoulder.

5) BE TRUE TO YOURSELF

I loved Star Wars when I was teenager, so I'm happy to write in that franchise. I never watched more than a few episodes of Star Trek, so to write a Star Trek novel would require a degree of research that I don't have the time, energy, or interest to muster. That, to me, would qualify as Selling Out.

On a similar note: although I am a big fan of Buffy and Angel, I don't believe I can write in the style required for that franchise. It's not that I wouldn't like to. I just know my limitations.

6) KNOW YOUR MARKET

Certain publishers license certain franchises, and certain franchises have a use-by date. There's no point writing the best *Captain Scarlet* tie-in novel ever when few people today remember the show.

7) EXPECT TO WORK HARD. VERY HARD

All commonsense stuff, in other words. Writing tie-in novels or novelisations is not for everyone, but it can be lucrative and satisfying work; it can generate enormous amounts of publicity; it can expose other work you have written to an entirely new audience. These are all good reasons for pursuing such a deal. The downsides are that you're working with someone else's core ideas, which you might find stifling, and that someone else has the final say on what appears in print; you retain no copyright over your work, and it will probably never be reviewed, except on Amazon and fan websites; the deadlines can be tight and the readership merciless.

With six Star Wars novels behind me, I can honestly say

that my career hasn't suffered for it, my bank account definitely enjoyed it, and best of all: I got a real rush out of it. If you'd told child-me that I'd be putting words in the mouths of Luke Skywalker and C-3PO, I would've said you were joking — but my eyes would've lit up at the thought. That light is still there — and at the end of that day, for every writer, however it got there, that's what counts.

Reach for the Stars

WITH THANKS TO JAMES BRADLEY, SIMON BROWN,
GARTH NIX, & JONATHAN STRAHAN

When I was your age, I wanted two things. Well, I wanted
more than just *two* things. There was a whole bunch of ways I
thought my life could have been better. School sucked, of
course, and so did my little sister. My name, too, was an
issue. Is there anyone else here who hates their name? It's
good to know you're not alone; maybe you could arrange a
trade afterwards. And if there's anyone here called "John
Silver", I hope you're happy. You've got the name I always
wanted.

Anyway, when it came to the future, there were two
things I specifically wanted. I wanted life to be a whole lot
more interesting than it was for me back then, and I wanted
to be taller.

Regarding the first point: I'd been reading science fiction
from a very young age, and you learn pretty fast when you
read that kind of stuff that the real world is plain dull in
comparison. There are no robots, no flying cars, no space
ships, no aliens, no lasers (not the shooting kind, anyway).
And if you read fantasy, there are no magic wands, no

dragons, no elves, no dwarves. There are no heroes waving swords and saving people.

My memory is pretty dim of those days, but I'm pretty sure I wanted to be a hero. Heroes have to be tall, hence the second wish. I'm not tall now, and obviously I was even shorter back then. That didn't stop me from dreaming. If there was any likelihood at all of heroes appearing, my chances would only be improved if I could gain an extra foot or so.

I never did amount to much, height-wise, and the heroes still haven't appeared, but I did keep on reading. And reading, and reading, and reading. And eventually I started writing, attempting quite blatantly to do what my favourite authors did: to tell a story that would keep readers entranced.

At an early age, I mastered the two first steps to being a writer, without even knowing I was doing it. The first is to read a lot. The second is to write a lot, and most importantly to write what you like reading. If you can do those two things, then any dreams you have of being a writer will come that much closer.

I didn't dream of being a writer back then. I was just dreaming of ways the world could be more interesting. The stories I wrote were full of all the things I wished I'd had. Bear in mind how long ago this was, by the way. There were no mobile phones or home computers back then. The Internet hadn't been invented. Cable TV, Nintendos, Sony walkmen, CDs, DVDs — even video players — were all in the future. If I'd been reading about *now* back then, I would've thought it was pretty cool.

I didn't have the imagination to see any of these things coming. Instead I wrote about lots of other cool things. I had space ships crashing into Jupiter; I had aliens trying to invade the Earth; I had giant spiders and a young boy with a fancy sword who could kill them. I was dreaming of a better life.

None of *these* things came true[1], but somehow I've managed to fall into a better life, almost by accident. The world may not have all the cool stuff I dreamed about back then, but I *do* make a living dreaming about the world as it could be — and that's the next best thing.

———

SCIENCE FICTION WRITER Gregory Benford describes his job has *dreaming in public.* 'These must be machine dreams,' he goes on to say, 'with gritty substance and some fact behind them' — but at their heart, they're still dreams. If we didn't dream, there would be no science fiction or fantasy stories — or horror stories either, for that matter, for nightmares are dreams too. And if people didn't want to dream, there'd be no one to read our stories. It works both ways.

I was ten years old when the first Star Wars movie came out: the one now called "Episode IV: A New Hope," in which Luke Skywalker inherits his father's lightsaber and Obi-Wan Kenobi is killed by his former apprentice. Even looking back on it now, that's a pretty impressive dream. As a kid, I was utterly infected. I saw the movie ten times at the cinema. I bought the book of the movie, and all the other books in the series. I listened to the soundtrack over and over again. I recorded the radio play every week as it went to air. I did a jigsaw with an X-wing shooting at a TIE fighter. If I could've signed up to become a Jedi Knight, I wouldn't have stopped to say goodbye to my family. I would have been out the door and on the landspeeder before you could say, 'I've got a bad feeling about this.'

For a few years, that world of Star Wars occupied a fair proportion of my dreaming time. Not all of it; there were other books and movies I liked, as is only healthy. But a significant chunk. I imagined stories and I put myself in them. If the World Wide Web had existed then, I almost certainly would have put some fanfic on-line — which probably would have been embarrassing to me now. Because they would have been terrible. I look back on my early work and cringe — but I'm glad I wrote it, because every word brought me one step closer to where I am now.

———

I SAID EARLIER that I didn't dream of being a writer back then. This seems amazing to me now, and maybe it seems strange to you, too, given where I am now. I wrote hundreds of thousands of words through late primary and high school, including three full-length novels and lots of smaller pieces. But it never occurred to me that I might do it for a living. I was just dreaming. By the time I was old enough to consider careers, I knew that writers earn a pittance, most of them, despite working horribly long hours, and they don't have such benefits as sick pay, leave loading, superannuation, and so on. Only a fool would take on a job like that. A fool or a dreamer.

The best advice I ever received was from a guy called Charles Brown. He founded and edited a long-running magazine called LOCUS, which all the world's SF& F writers read to find out what's happening in the field. He was a big deal, in other words, and he came to talk to a bunch of new writers who'd won prizes in something called the Writers of the Future Contest.

I was among those new writers. This was ten years ago, when I'd already decided to try to be a writer, but hadn't written any novels yet, or made much money at all. I was just hammering away at it because there was nothing else I wanted to do badly enough. The thought of spending most of my life doing something I hated, like being a doctor or a lawyer, was just unbearable.

Anyway, Charles sat us down and congratulated us on our success. It was pretty cool, he said; we should be proud of getting this far because not many people do. Of every hundred people who want to write, only one goes on to do something about it, to actually try writing something. If you take a hundred of those people who actually do something about it, whether it's write a few poems or the beginning of a novel, only one in that hundred actually finishes anything. And if you take a hundred of those finishers, only one of them will actually sell their work professionally.

If you add up all the zeroes, that means that just one wannabe writer in a million will sell or win an award for their story, poem or novel. So sitting around that table of prize-winners really *was* something to be proud of.

But that wasn't the end of it. If you take a hundred people who have sold a professional story, poem or novel, how many of them are likely to ever make a career out of writing? That is, how many will take that one pro sale and turn it into a regular income on which they can support themselves indefinitely?

Just one.

Well, I looked around the table. There were around twenty of us in the room, and we were all high on that the thought that we were *real* writers now. All our stories were going to win prizes, and our novels would all bestsellers.

It doesn't work like that, Charlie said. If the odds are one in a hundred, then the chances were that *none* of us in that room were going to get anywhere. Oh, we might sell a few more stories, here and there. Maybe a novel, if we were lucky. But earn enough to make a living from it? Unlikely.

It would be better, he said, if we gave up right now. Saved

ourselves the years of hardship and heartbreak. Put all that wasted energy into a career that would actually make money, and spare our families and loved ones all that frustration and anger when we didn't ultimately get anywhere. How many zeroes are we up to now? For every *one hundred million* people who dream of being a writer, there's just one who reaps the rewards. What makes you think you're going to be that one?

I listened to him and thought, "He's making perfect sense. Everything he says is true. It makes me feel sick inside to admit it, but I *am* crazy for thinking I might get anywhere. I know the odds are stacked against me, and only either pride or stupidity — or both — has got me this far. The bubble is bound to pop eventually, as it will for ninety-nine million, nine hundred and ninety-nine thousand, nine hundred and ninety-eight other wannabe writers. And one lucky one will go on, not knowing just how lucky they are. Damn them."

It took me the rest of his speech to realise that, although Charles was absolutely right, it didn't change one thing. The odds were still awful; I was an idiot for even trying. But I would be that one in one hundred million if I had to sweat blood to do it, and I would love every moment of it. I would prove Charles Brown absolutely right by doing the exact opposite of what he told me to do.

And I did.

When I was younger, I dreamed. I reached for the stars. When I was older, I realised that dreaming and reaching wasn't enough. I had to do more than just lie there, looking upward and wishing. If I *didn't* do more than that, I wouldn't get anywhere at all.

———

ANOTHER WRITER, Kevin J Anderson, borrowed a saying that I like to share in turn with new writers: 'The harder I work,' he says, 'the luckier I get.' Sometimes I think that's the wisest thing anyone has ever said, writers included. Forget all that stuff about writing from the heart, or writing what you know. That comes with practice. Work hard at what you love; make your own luck. Whether it's skateboard, painting, football, or writing, those words apply: if you're passionate about it and you're prepared to give it your all, then you'll increase your chances of getting a lucky break along the way.

The trick, I guess, is to find the thing you love. It's all very well for me to stand up here and tell you that this is what you have to do. I mean, I've found my thing. What if yours takes a long time to find? Or you haven't come across it yet? What if your thing is Swedish ice-sculpture and you've never left Adelaide? What happens then?

I don't know. But I *do* know that being afraid of trying will only hold you back. If you'd told me when I was a kid that I would end up writing Star Wars novels and other books, I would've told you that you were mad — not because I didn't want to do it, but because I assumed I never had a chance.

If I'd never tried, I never would've made it, and neither would any of the other writers assembled here tonight.

But here we are, young writers and old, dreaming for a living. We don't have friends or relatives telling us off or thinking we're weird for sticking our heads into books all the time, like I did when I was younger, because now it's what we do. It's our job. We have to do it, and it's hard work, most of the time. On the odd occasions when it doesn't feel like a job at all, when it takes me across the world to places like Hollywood Boulevard and Skywalker Ranch — at times like that, I have to remind myself that, like all writers, I've *earned* the fun parts. They don't just happen by magic; we didn't win them in a lottery. We made our own luck; we proved, whether we knew it or not, Charles Brown right.

You could be one of us, one day. Don't let anybody tell you can't do it. They're only right if you believe them. Maybe the next *one in one hundred million* is sitting in this room right now. If you are, don't forget to reach for the stars, and always expect to do a lot of climbing to get there. Astronauts have to train for years before they go up in a space shuttle. I may not have actually gone to the stars, but in my head I have a million times or more — and that really is the next best thing.

---

1. Actually, one of these things did come true. Not the giant spiders, thank goodness.

Addendum

A lot of the advice in these essays is contingent on factors beyond the scope of this collection. That doesn't mean it can't still be true sometimes — and *some* of the advice is *always* true. I'm referring to little gems like:

- be professional
- work hard
- be true to yourself
- find your own definition of success
- expect things to change because they always will

These don't need qualification, because they apply to all writers at every stage of their career. They are, if you like, the first principles from which all other nuggets of writing advice evolve. Rules, perhaps. Or commandments.

You'll find my list of my "10.5 Commandments of Writing" online at The Conversation. Here's a link: https://theconversation.com/profiles/sean-williams-794459

About the Author

Sean Williams was born in the dry, flat lands of South Australia, where he still lives with his wife and family and a pet plastic fish. He has been called many things in his time, including (somewhat ostentatiously) "the premier Australian speculative fiction writer of the age" (Aurealis), the "Emperor of Sci-Fi" (Adelaide Advertiser), the "Lord of the Genre" (Perth Writers' Festival), and the "King of Chameleons" (Australian Book Review) for the diversity of his published output. That output includes over forty novels for readers all ages, one hundred-plus short stories across numerous genres, the odd published poem, and even a sci-fi musical. He also likes making up new words. He is a multiple recipient of the Aurealis and Ditmar Awards and has been nominated for the Philip K. Dick Award, the Seiun Award, and the William Atheling Jr. Award for criticism. He received the "SA Great" Literature Award in 2000 and the Peter McNamara Award for contributions to Australian speculative fiction in 2008. His latest series are *Troubletwisters*, a fantasy for middle grade readers co-written with Garth Nix, and *Twinmaker*, a near-future thriller for young adults (and old adults too). Over forty bonus short stories set in the Twinmaker universe are available online. In

2014, Sean and Garth co-authored the third novel in the New York Times bestselling Spirit Animals series, *Blood Ties*.

facebook.com/seanwilliamsauthor

twitter.com/adelaidesean

instagram.com/adelaidesean

amazon.com/Sean-Williams

goodreads.com/seanwilliams

Also by Sean Williams

Series

The Books of the Change

The Books of the Cataclysm

The Broken Land

Astropolis

Twinmaker

The Fixers

Star Wars: The Force Unleashed

Troubletwisters (with Garth Nix)

Have Sword, Will Travel (with Garth Nix)

Evergence (with Shane Dix)

Orphans (with Shane Dix)

Geodesica (with Shane Dix)

Star Wars: New Jedi Order: Force Heretic (with Shane Dix)

-

Standalone novels

Metal Fatigue

The Resurrected Man

Her Perilous Mansion

Spirit Animals: Blood Ties (with Garth Nix)

Star Wars: The Old Republic: Fatal Alliance

www.ingramcontent.com/pod-product-compliance
Lightning Source LLC
Chambersburg PA
CBHW022106020426
42335CB00012B/858